# WHO WOULD WIN?®

## JAGUAR

## VS.

## SKUNK

### BY
### JERRY PALLOTTA
#### ILLUSTRATED BY
#### ROB BOLSTER

## Scholastic Inc.

*The publisher would like to thank the following for their
kind permission to use their photographs in this book:
Photos ©: 1 center right: Isselee/Dreamstime; 4: anankkml/Thinkstock;
5: Isselee/Dreamstime; 6 bottom: André Baertschi/wildtropix.com;
16 bottom: Fabiofersa/Dreamstime; 20 top: krinkog/Fotolia;
21 bottom: Courtesy Skunk Works® Lockheed Martin Corporation;
24 center: Julesuyttenbroeck/Dreamstime; 29 top: Panoramic Images/Getty Images.*

*Thank you to Barbara Burns and all my pals at Norfolk Academy.*
— *J.P.*

*Dedicated to all who make their living on the ocean.*
— *R.B.*

Text copyright © 2017 by Jerry Pallotta.
Illustrations copyright © 2017 by Rob Bolster.

ISBN 978-0-545-94608-7

10 9 8 7 6                                                                        18 19 20 21

Printed in the U.S.A.                                                                    40
First printing, 2017

What would happen if a skunk and a jaguar came nose to nose? If they had a fight, who do you think would win?

# MEET THE JAGUAR

The jaguar is a mammal in the cat family. It is the third-largest cat on Earth. The jaguar is a skilled hunter and an excellent swimmer. Its scientific name is *Panthera onca*.

### DEFINITION
*A mammal is a warm-blooded animal that often has hair or fur.*

### BIG FACT
*The Siberian tiger is the largest of all cats.*

### SECOND FACT
*The lion is the second-largest cat.*

# MEET THE SKUNK

The skunk is a mammal in the Mephitidae family. A striped skunk's scientific name is *Mephitis mephitis*, which means "bad smell." Skunks have black-and-white fur.

**FACT**
*The word "skunk" comes from the Algonquin Indian language.*

The skunk is not known for its scary teeth or sharp claws. It is famous because it can make a stink!

# CLIMB

Jaguars can climb trees. They often drag their freshly killed prey up into the branches of a tree.

# SWIM

Most cats do not like to go in the water, but the jaguar is an excellent swimmer. Watch out, crocodiles! Watch out, turtles!

# HIDE

The skunk is good at hiding. It is rarely seen during daylight. Where is the skunk?

**NOISY FACT**
*If you hear an animal on your roof, it's probably a raccoon or a squirrel, not a skunk.*

**QUESTION**
*Have you ever smelled a skunk in your neighborhood?*

Under the house? In the trash can? Over there by the bushes?

# KNOW YOUR CAT FUR

### jaguar: rosettes

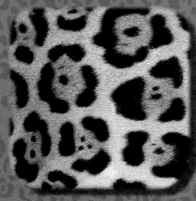

### leopard: c-shaped spots

### cheetah: polka dots

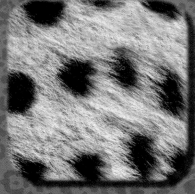

### tiger: stripes

### lion: plain

# KNOW YOUR STRIPES

zorilla

hog-nosed skunk

spotted skunk

hooded skunk

**FURRY FACT**
*Baby skunks are born with stripes.*

striped skunk

This is a stinky page! In this book we will feature the striped skunk.

# RANGE

The jaguar lives in much of Central America and South America.

NORTH AMERICA

PACIFIC OCEAN

ATLANTIC OCEAN

CENTRAL AMERICA

SOUTH AMERICA

jaguar territory

**FACT**
*Jaguars do not live in Africa.*

Many jaguars live in rain forests. They also hunt on grassland and savannas.

# WORLD

Skunks are found on every continent except Antarctica
and Australia.

ARCTIC OCEAN

EUROPE

ASIA

PACIFIC
OCEAN

AFRICA

INDIAN
OCEAN

skunk
territory

AUSTRALIA

SOUTHERN OCEAN

ANTARCTICA

# CREPUSCULAR

The jaguar sometimes is a crepuscular hunter.

**DEFINITION**
*"Crepuscular" means an animal hunts at dawn and at dusk.*

**AUTO FACT**
*There is a famous sports car called the Jaguar.*

Dawn is when the sun first rises. Dusk is when the sun sets

**TIME-OF-DAY FACTS**
*Dawn is also called daybreak. Dusk is also called twilight.*

# NOCTURNAL

The skunk is a nocturnal hunter. It comes out at night.

**SKUNK IDIOM**

To "get skunked" sometimes means to go fishing and not catch anything.

"Hey, Rob, maybe we should write a nocturnal alphabet book." —Jerry

The **NOCTURNAL** Alphabet Book

BY
JERRY PALLOTTA
ILLUSTRATED BY
ROB BOLSTER
■SCHOLASTIC

# DINNER

Zoologists studied jaguars and discovered that they eat dozens of different types of animals.

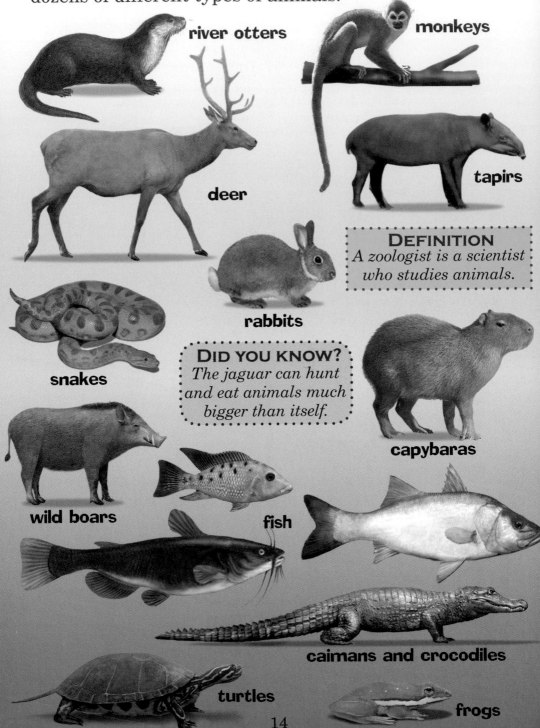

river otters

monkeys

deer

tapirs

**DEFINITION**
*A zoologist is a scientist who studies animals.*

rabbits

snakes

**DID YOU KNOW?**
*The jaguar can hunt and eat animals much bigger than itself.*

capybaras

wild boars

fish

caimans and crocodiles

turtles

frogs

14

# SUPPER

Skunks are omnivores. They eat plants and animals. A skunk would gladly eat spaghetti or a cheeseburger, too.

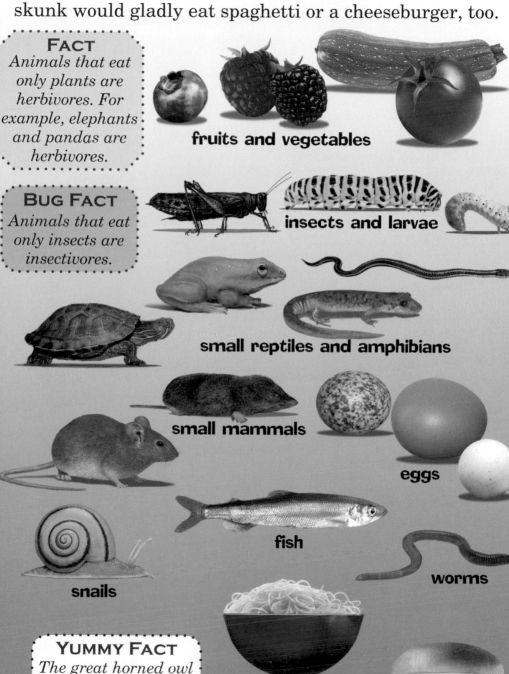

fruits and vegetables

insects and larvae

small reptiles and amphibians

small mammals

eggs

fish

snails

worms

spaghetti

cheeseburger

# WARNING
# BEWARE THE JAGUAR

The jaguar is a magnificent creature. If there were an animal Olympics, the jaguar might win the gold medal for hunting.

However, the jaguar is not a gentle animal. It stalks and ambushes its prey. Its jaws are so strong it can bite turtle shells, pierce skulls, and crush necks.

### TAIL FACT
*The jaguar has the shortest tail of all the big cats; the snow leopard has the longest tail.*

# WARNING BEWARE THE SKUNK

One day, a skunk sprayed the underside of a car. The car smelled so bad the family couldn't drive it for a week. Stinky!

**FACT**
*A skunk will not spray another skunk.*

A skunk was near a home's outdoor air-conditioning unit. The skunk got startled and sprayed. The smell went through the central air vents in the house, and the people couldn't live there for a month. It wasn't funny!

**FACT**
*If you see a skunk during daylight, it is usually a sick skunk.*

A girl got sprayed by a skunk on her way to school. The principal sent her home. To get the skunk smell off, she had to take a bath in tomato juice. Her parents had to throw her clothes away.

**FACT**
*Skunk spray is not poisonous.*

# HEAR

How might you know a jaguar is in the area? You would hear it! The jaguar is the only cat in the Western Hemisphere that roars.

**MEOW FACT**
*House cats meow.
Lions, tigers, leopards,
and jaguars roar!*

# SMELL

How would you know a skunk is in the area? You might smell it! Yuck! The skunk's smell comes from glands near its tail. The skunk lifts its tail and shoots its stinky mist.

### FACT

*Skunks are less likely to spray if they can't see what they are spraying. If a pest-removal worker catches a skunk in a cage, he might cover the cage with a blanket so the skunk won't spray.*

# ALONE

The jaguar is a solitary cat. It is perfectly happy living alone.

**DEFINITION**
*"Solitary" and "solo" both mean "alone."*

This might be what it would look like if jaguars hunted in a pack. Yikes!

**SOLO FACT**
*The tiger is a solitary hunter.*

**PACK FACT**
*The lion is a pack hunter.*

# COOL SMELLY FACTS

The name "Chicago" is from the Ojibwa Indian language for "skunk land."

**CHICAGO SKYLINE**

*DID YOU KNOW?*
*Skunk cabbage smells like skunk spray.*

Skunk Works® was the secret name of the Lockheed Martin aircraft factory in Palmdale, California, which built the top secret U-2 spy plane, the SR-71 Blackbird, the F-117 Nighthawk stealth fighter, and the F-22 Raptor.

# TEETH

The jaguar has teeth that are perfect for catching and eating meat.

**DID YOU KNOW?**
*The last teeth on the upper jaw of every cat are sideways.*

## HEIGHT AND WEIGHT

36 INCHES

26"-30" HIGH AT SHOULDER

24

12

0

**WEIGHT**
*120–210 pounds*

# LITTLE JAW

The skunk has small teeth, but they do the job!

**DID YOU KNOW?**
*A skunk's smell is made up of seven chemicals.*

**DID YOU KNOW?**
*Some skunks do handstands so they appear larger.*

## LENGTH AND WEIGHT

INCHES
0    12    24    36

22"-31" LONG

**WEIGHT**
4–12 pounds

# MORE WEAPONS

The jaguar has other weapons besides its huge teeth and strong jaws.

## SHARP CLAWS

## CAMOUFLAGE

## SPEED/QUICKNESS

Wow! A jaguar can run fifty miles per hour. That is really moving!

# ONE WEAPON

Maybe all you need is one secret weapon. The skunk's ability to create a terrible smell has kept it safe for millions of years.

> ### DID YOU KNOW?
> *The skunk can shoot its spray up to six times in a row before it runs out.*

> ### FACT
> *Skunk spray is highly flammable.*

## STINK

Skunks aren't fast. But they are experts in chemical warfare.

The jaguar sneaks up on a napping crocodile and crushes its neck with one giant bite!

As the jaguar was eating the crocodile, the skunk found a tasty dragonfly.